FROGS, TOADS, LIZARDS, and SALAMANDERS

NANCY WINSLOW PARKER
AND
JOAN RICHARDS WRIGHT

Illustrations by Nancy Winslow Parker

GREENWILLOW BOOKS, NEW YORK

NOTE

The scientific symbols for male, ♂, and female, ♀, are used throughout the book. The line ⊢——⊣ denotes the maximum adult length of the frog or toad from snout to vent and of the lizard or salamander from snout to tip of tail. Larger measurements are indicated by inches and feet. Each subject's common and scientific names are given. In the scientific name, the first word is the genus; the second is the species; the third denotes subspecies. The color of most amphibians and reptiles is variable depending on temperature, environment, age, sex, and activity. The symbol N stands for nocturnal, D for diurnal.

Frogs, toads, lizards, and salamanders are much happier in their native habitats. They eat only live things and may starve in captivity. It is best that they be left in their natural environment.

A black pen line was combined with watercolor paints and colored pencils for the full-color art.
The typefaces are Sabon and Symbol.

Text copyright © 1990 by Nancy Winslow Parker and Joan Richards Wright.
Illustrations copyright © 1990 by Nancy Winslow Parker.
Printed in Singapore by Tien Wah Press   First Edition   10 9 8 7

Library of Congress Cataloging-in-Publication Data
Parker, Nancy Winslow.   Frogs, toads, lizards, and salamanders.
Bibliography: p.   Includes index.   Summary: Describes the physical characteristics, habits, and natural environment of a variety of frogs, toads, lizards, and salamanders. 1. Frogs—Juvenile literature. 2. Toads—Juvenile literature. 3. Lizards—Juvenile literature. 4. Salamanders—Juvenile literature. [1. Frogs. 2. Toads. 3. Lizards. 4. Salamanders]   I. Wright, Joan Richards.   II. Title.   QL668.E2P287
1990   597.6   89-11686   ISBN 0-688-08680-2   ISBN 0-688-08681-0 (lib. bdg.)

For Professor William M. Ingram,
Mills College, California, 1941–1952
—N. W. P.

For L. L. R. and S. D. R.
—J. R. W.

With thanks to Michael W. Klemens, Department of
Herpetology, American Museum of Natural History,
who was the consultant for this book.

Wet Bullfrog tracks
showing body and thigh print,
and toed-in feet
hitting the ground.

Contents

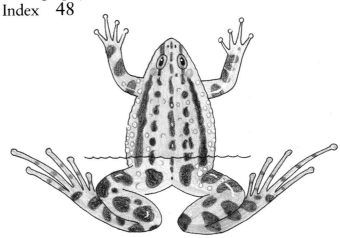

Nick saw a Hellbender
in the brook
when he bent down
to check his hook.

HELLBENDER

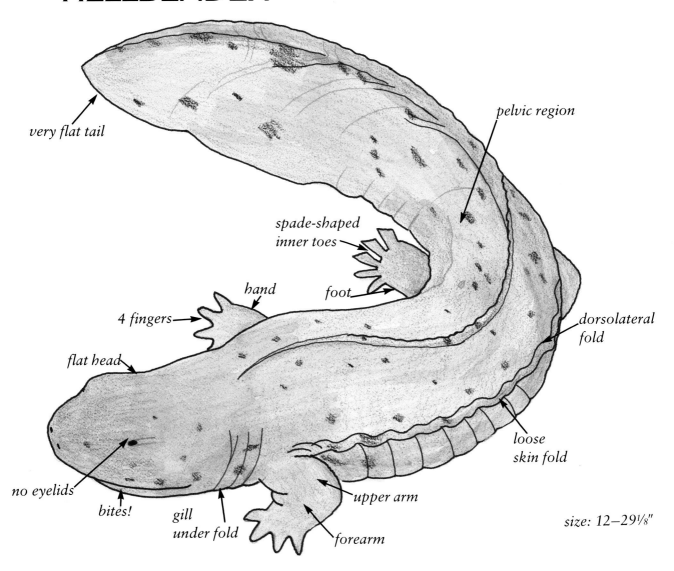

very flat tail

pelvic region

spade-shaped
inner toes

foot

hand

4 fingers

dorsolateral
fold

flat head

no eyelids

bites!

gill
under fold

upper arm

loose
skin fold

forearm

size: 12–29⅛"

HELLBENDER (*Cryptobranchus alleganiensis*) N

Nick knew that this large, ugly-looking salamander is usually harmless. The aquatic Hellbender lives in rocky streams, where the rapidly moving water makes it difficult to deposit eggs safely. The female lays up to 500 eggs in long, tangled strings, which the male fertilizes by spraying. The male guards the nest but sometimes eats the eggs. Hellbenders eat crayfish, worms, snails, fish eggs, and insects. They may live up to 55 years in captivity. Scientists do not know the life span of most amphibians in the wild.

7

Peeking from Grant's sailor suit was a California Newt.

CALIFORNIA NEWT

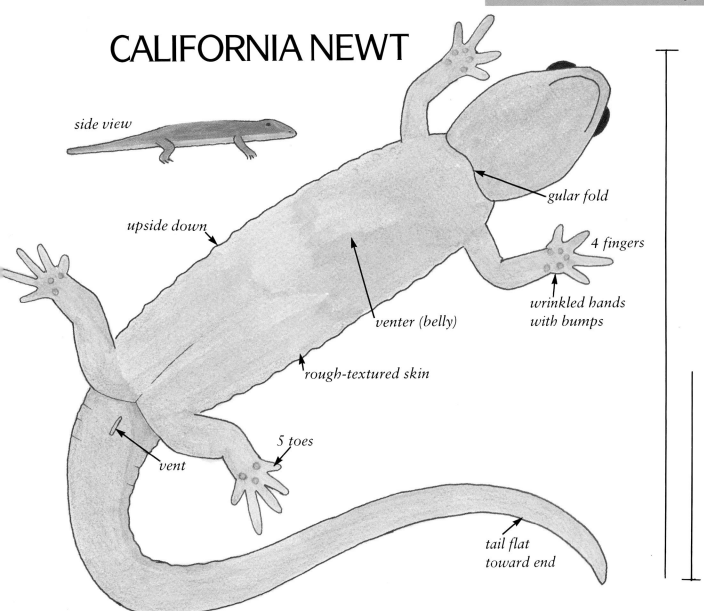

side view

upside down

gular fold

venter (belly)

4 fingers

wrinkled hands with bumps

rough-textured skin

vent

5 toes

tail flat toward end

CALIFORNIA NEWT *(Taricha torosa)* Ⓝ Ⓓ

Floating in a tire tube, Grant did not see the hidden newt. The California Newt begins life in a clutch of up to 24 eggs deposited on a water plant. The larvae live in water. Within months they become terrestrial creatures. They live in damp places and around forest ponds and streams, where they mature to adulthood. They return to water to breed. During dry weather, California Newts live under damp tree leaves or in other animals' burrows. When a California Newt is angry or threatened, it arches its tail over its back, exposing its deep orange underbelly to warn predators away.

9

A slimy Two-toed Amphiuma
terrified Grant's aunt from Yuma.

TWO-TOED AMPHIUMA

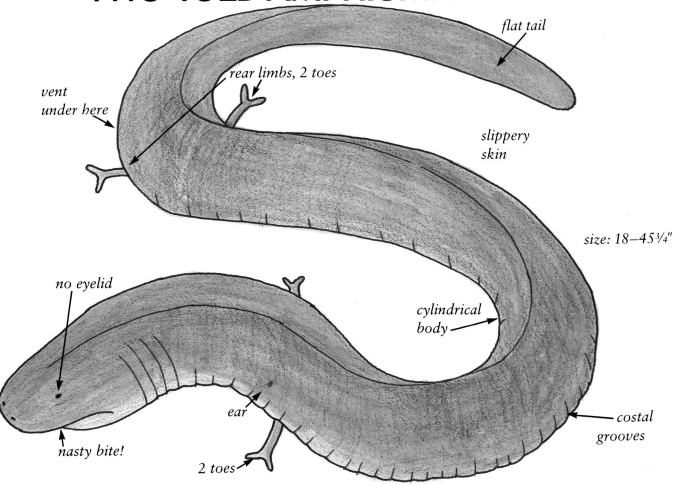

flat tail

rear limbs, 2 toes

vent under here

slippery skin

size: 18–45¾"

no eyelid

cylindrical body

ear

nasty bite!

2 toes

costal grooves

TWO-TOED AMPHIUMA *(Amphiuma means)* N

Grant's aunt was picking flowers by a drainage ditch occupied by a fat, snakelike Two-toed Amphiuma. Amphiumas are aquatic. Their under-developed legs are of little use except to the larval amphiumas in helping them move along the river bottom. Amphiumas live in rivers, streams, swamps, bayous, and drainage ditches. Occasionally they leave the water during wet weather, but their skin must stay moist. Up to 60 costal grooves along the length of their bodies move water, by capillary action, to the upper skin surface. They dig their burrows in the soft, muddy river bottom. They forage in the shallow water for fish, crayfish, frogs, snakes, and smaller amphiumas. The female lays about 50 to 100 eggs in looped strings. They hatch in about 5 months. An amphiuma is known to have lived more than 14 years in captivity.

11

Doug let out an awful wail
when the Ensatina lost its tail.

LARGE-BLOTCHED ENSATINA

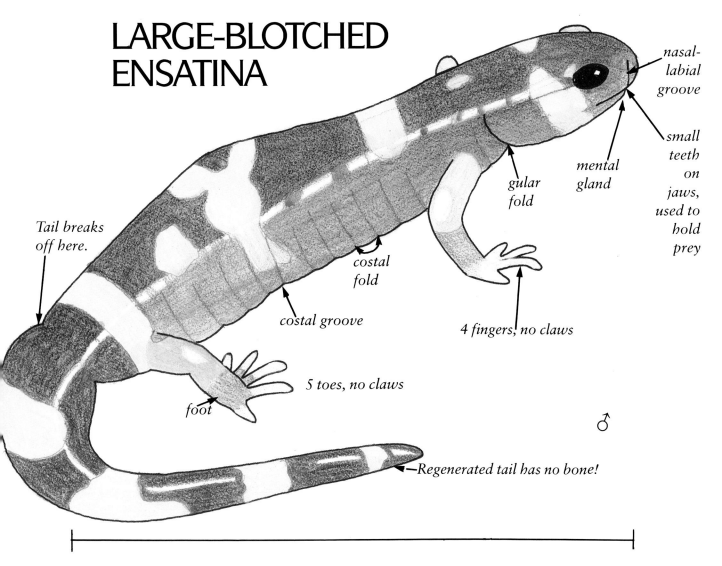

nasal-labial groove

small teeth on jaws, used to hold prey

mental gland

gular fold

Tail breaks off here.

costal fold

costal groove

4 fingers, no claws

5 toes, no claws

foot

♂

Regenerated tail has no bone!

LARGE-BLOTCHED ENSATINA
(Ensatina eschscholtzi klauberi)

[N]

Doug had grabbed the Ensatina by its tail. He did not know that the tail of the Ensatina, like the tails of many other salamanders, breaks off when it is grabbed or roughly handled. The separated tail wiggles about, distracting the enemy while the salamander escapes. Another tail will grow back. The Ensatina also protects itself from enemies by standing stiff-legged, showing its belly, swinging its tail, and looking fierce. The Ensatina, a lungless salamander, breathes through its skin. Ensatinas live in damp, shady evergreen forests. In the spring the Ensatina lays about 15 eggs that hatch the following fall. Ensatinas live as long as 10 to 15 years.

13

Nick's dog chased a Spadefoot Toad down the dark, deserted road.

EASTERN SPADEFOOT TOAD

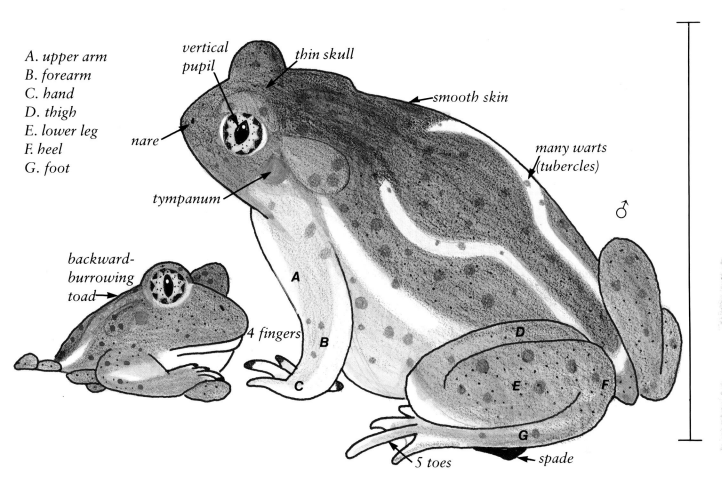

A. *upper arm*
B. *forearm*
C. *hand*
D. *thigh*
E. *lower leg*
F. *heel*
G. *foot*

vertical pupil
thin skull
smooth skin
nare
many warts (tubercles)
tympanum
backward-burrowing toad
4 fingers
5 toes
spade
♂

EASTERN SPADEFOOT TOAD
(Scaphiopus holbrooki holbrooki)

N

Because it was dark and wet, there was a Spadefoot Toad around for Nick's dog to chase. Spadefoot Toads spend the daytime hours in their burrows several feet underground. A hard, crescent-shaped spade on each hind foot is a critical tool for these marathon diggers. Spadefoot Toads will turn around and around while digging backward and disappear magically into the earth. During the fast-paced breeding season, normally solitary Spadefoot Toads become very sociable. They gather noisily in large groups after a rainfall to check out breeding pools and puddles and potential mates. In ponds Spadefoot Toad tadpoles move their tails back and forth to stir up any edible debris. Spadefoot Toads eat beetles, crickets, spiders, other small insects and worms.

15

Onto Patty's pie à la mode
hopped a large American Toad.

AMERICAN TOAD

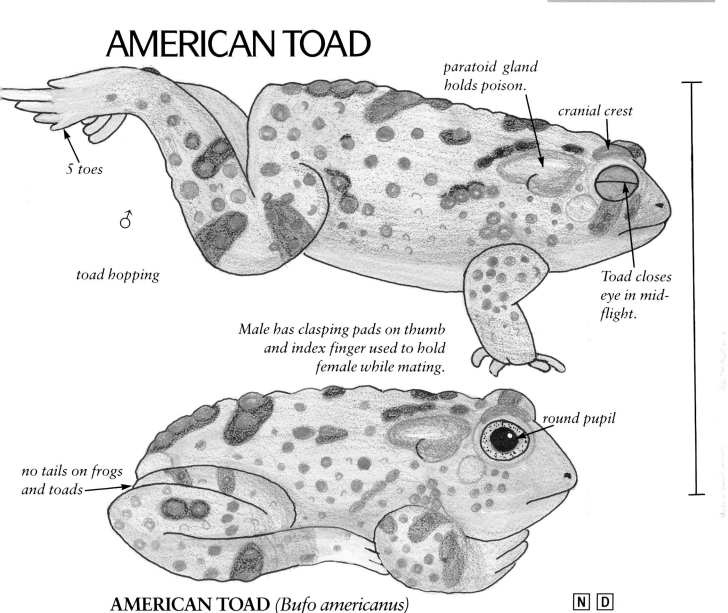

5 toes

♂

toad hopping

paratoid gland
holds poison.

cranial crest

Toad closes
eye in mid-
flight.

Male has clasping pads on thumb
and index finger used to hold
female while mating.

round pupil

no tails on frogs
and toads

AMERICAN TOAD *(Bufo americanus)* N D

The toad that landed in Patty's ice cream lives in woods and backyards in moist places. The American Toad has a huge appetite. A toad, in fact, can eat 86 flies in 10 minutes, several thousand insects in a month, and 2,000 cutworms during a summer, a great help to people in controlling pests. The American Toad breeds in early spring. The male's flutelike courtship trill is especially beautiful. Except during breeding, toads lead solitary lives in their favorite spots. A European Toad *(Bufo bufo)*, a close cousin of the American Toad, is known to have lived under the steps in an English country garden for 36 years, emerging punctually every evening for a hop around its home.

An Oak Toad watched
from the riverbank
as Rita's boat
capsized and sank.

OAK TOAD

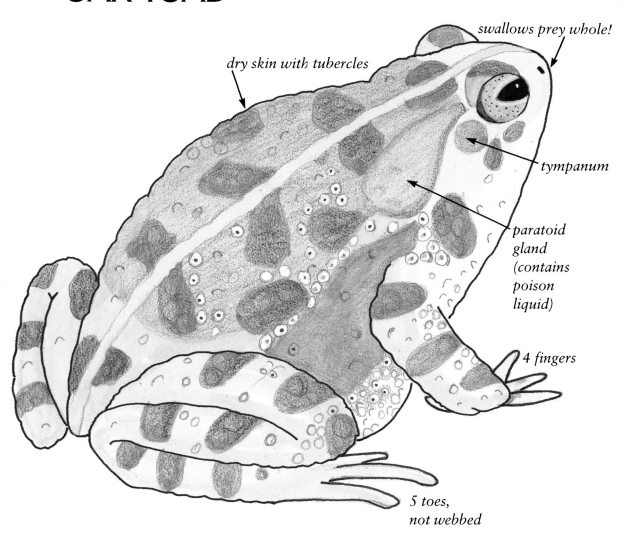

swallows prey whole!

dry skin with tubercles

tympanum

paratoid gland (contains poison liquid)

4 fingers

5 toes, not webbed

OAK TOAD *(Bufo quercicus)* 　D

The tiny Oak Toad observing Rita's disaster is the smallest toad in North America. Some may be less than an inch long. As with most toads, the primary diet of the Oak Toad is live insects—and lots of them! Toads will not eat anything that doesn't move. The toad doesn't even begin to consider an insect meal until it is within "tongue range." Then its sticky, fast tongue flicks out and grabs the insect. As it swallows, its eyeballs move back into the roof of its mouth and push the food farther down toward the toad's stomach. A toad uses its front feet to remove unpleasant things from its mouth and to stuff in bigger things, like worms.

Ben hardly knew
what to do
when a Texas Toad
fell out of his shoe.

TEXAS TOAD

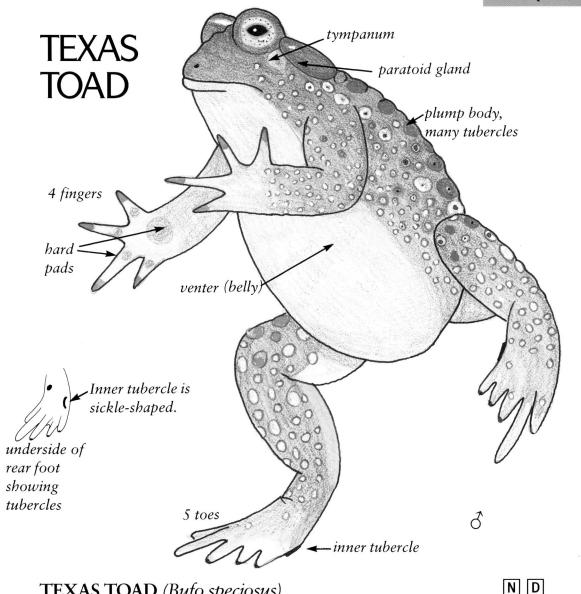

tympanum

paratoid gland

plump body, many tubercles

4 fingers

hard pads

venter (belly)

Inner tubercle is sickle-shaped.

underside of rear foot showing tubercles

5 toes

inner tubercle

♂

TEXAS TOAD *(Bufo speciosus)* N D

The Texas Toad borrowed Ben's shoe for a cozy nap. When toads are threatened, they like to play dead. Other toads inflate themselves when faced with danger, and some hop away wildly. The poison released by a toad's paratoid glands is another important defense. The poison irritates the mouth and throat of the predator. The paratoid glands of the Colorado River Toad *(Bufo alvarius)* have a more toxic poison, strong enough to kill a dog. A toad, like most amphibians, sheds its skin. The process begins as a giant yawn. The toad twists, bends, stretches, and contorts its body in amazing ways to loosen the shedding skin. Finally, the toad pulls the skin completely off, stuffs it into its mouth, and swallows it.

While picking berries
near the bog,
Thelma found
a big Bullfrog.

BULLFROG

Upper eyelid cannot close; lower lid comes up.

nare

tympanum (external eardrum) male 1.5 x eye width

tiny teeth, top and bottom

sacral hump

worm

yellow throat in male

size: 3½–8"

A. *upper arm*
B. *forearm*
C. *wrist*
D. *hand*
E. *fingers (4)*
F. *thigh*
G. *lower leg*
H. *heel*
I. *foot*
J. *toes (5)*

no webbing on last joint of longest toe

♂

BULLFROG (*Rana catesbeiana*) N D

Thelma probably surprised the Bullfrog when she wandered into its "turf." The Bullfrog is the largest frog in North America. It takes up to 5 years to become an adult, depending on the climate. Bullfrogs will eat almost anything that moves and is smaller than they are, even a duckling. The Bullfrog doesn't like to stalk its prey, preferring to sit and wait until the victim appears. It does not congregate in large groups during breeding season. It usually waits in its own pond until the right mate appears. It is at home in the water and, although it is an amphibian, the adult Bullfrog rarely goes on land. The Bullfrog's call is a low-pitched *jug-o-rum*.

23

Rita tripped on a fallen log,
trying to catch a Leopard Frog.

SOUTHERN LEOPARD FROG

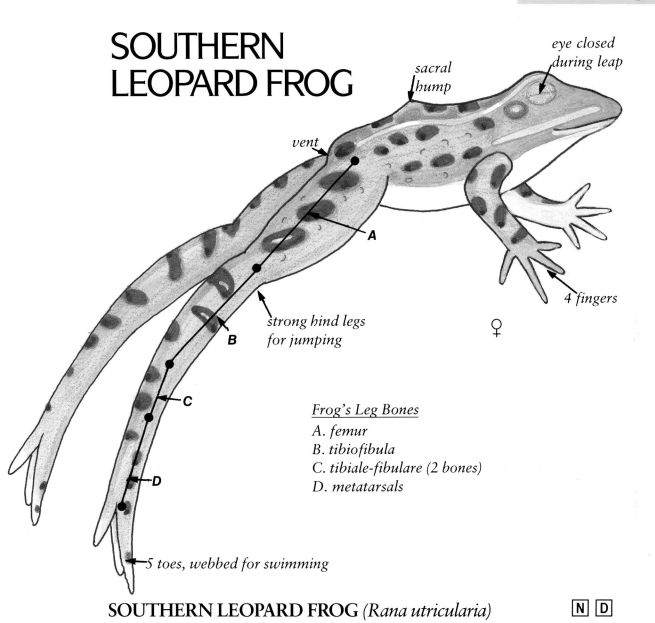

sacral hump

eye closed during leap

vent

A

strong hind legs for jumping

B

C

D

♀

4 fingers

Frog's Leg Bones
A. *femur*
B. *tibiofibula*
C. *tibiale-fibulare (2 bones)*
D. *metatarsals*

5 toes, webbed for swimming

SOUTHERN LEOPARD FROG (*Rana utricularia*)   N D

Rita and Thelma were trying to catch a Southern Leopard Frog for their science class. The Southern Leopard Frog can execute quick turns underwater after a dive and fool predators by coming up in a totally unexpected place. A sitting frog's legs are folded into 3 sections. When the legs are extended to jump, powerful muscles uncoil like a spring, enabling the frog to jump as much as 10 times its body length. The shorter front legs act as shock absorbers as the frog lands. Frogs hold some great jumping records. The longest frog jump on record—a whopping 20 feet 3⅜ inches—was made by "Weird Harold" in 1984 at California's Calaveras County Jumping Frog Jubilee.

While walking by
the pond one day,
Nick saw some
Chorus Frogs at play.

SOUTHERN CHORUS FROG

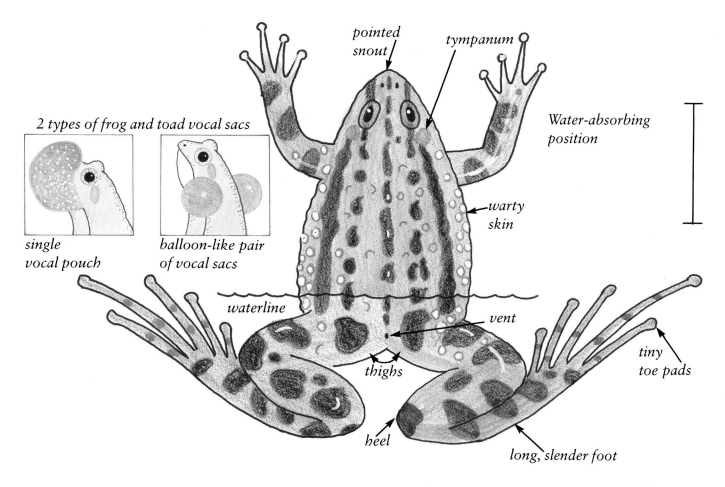

2 types of frog and toad vocal sacs

single
vocal pouch

balloon-like pair
of vocal sacs

pointed
snout

tympanum

Water-absorbing
position

warty
skin

waterline

vent

thighs

tiny
toe pads

heel

long, slender foot

SOUTHERN CHORUS FROG (*Pseudacris nigrita*) N

Nick was lucky to see Southern Chorus Frogs during the day because, like most treefrogs, they are primarily nocturnal. Treefrogs are small. Most treefrogs are better climbers and walkers than they are jumpers. The toes of most treefrogs have suction pads to help them climb. The call is a raspy trill. The voice of a frog or toad is sometimes the *only* way to tell one species from another. The males sing in chorus to attract a mate. Only males have well-developed voices. Frogs do not drink. They absorb water through the skin on their thighs and lower abdomens. Frogs and toads breed each spring in definite order. In the Boston area, for instance, the Wood Frog breeds in mid-March, followed by, on subsequent dates, the Leopard Frog, American Toad, Pickerel Frog, Fowler's Toad, Gray Treefrog, and, finally, the Bullfrog in June or July.

Nina covered
with bandannas
her three
African Platannas.

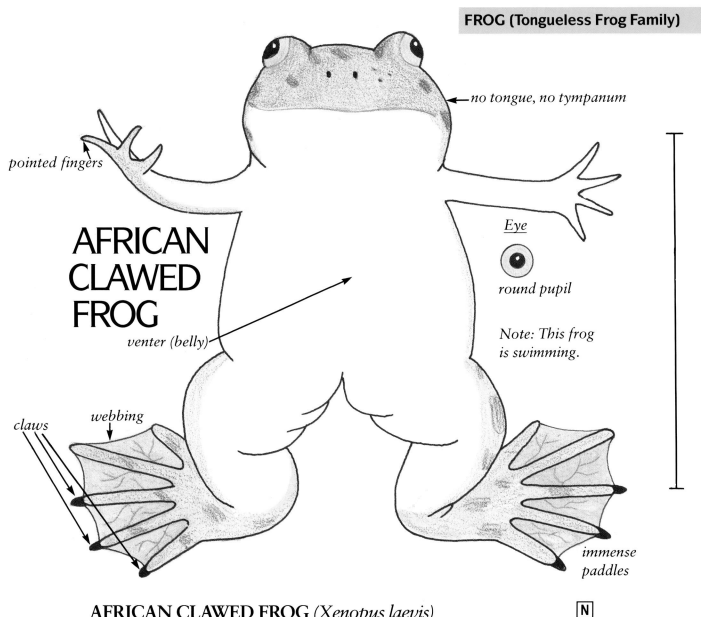

no tongue, no tympanum

pointed fingers

AFRICAN
CLAWED
FROG

venter (belly)

Eye

round pupil

Note: This frog
is swimming.

claws

webbing

immense
paddles

AFRICAN CLAWED FROG *(Xenopus laevis)* [N]

Nina's African Clawed Frogs, also known as Platannas, have no tongues, no
teeth, and no external eardrums. They are native to Africa and are sold in the
United States as pets. The Platannas in California are descendants of released
pets. A Platanna uses its fingers to catch prey and to stuff food into its mouth. In
the wild, it consumes great quantities of mosquito eggs and larvae, helping
control malaria. The Platanna has long, strong, muscular legs and huge webbed
feet with sharp black claws on 3 of its toes. The claws are used to hold on to
branches in fast-running streams, to create a defensive smoke screen by stirring
up mud on river bottoms, and to dig into damp places when streams are dry.
This frog is a champion swimmer but moves rather clumsily on land.

Under Grandma's
Persian rugs,
a hungry Gecko
looks for bugs.

MEDITERRANEAN GECKO

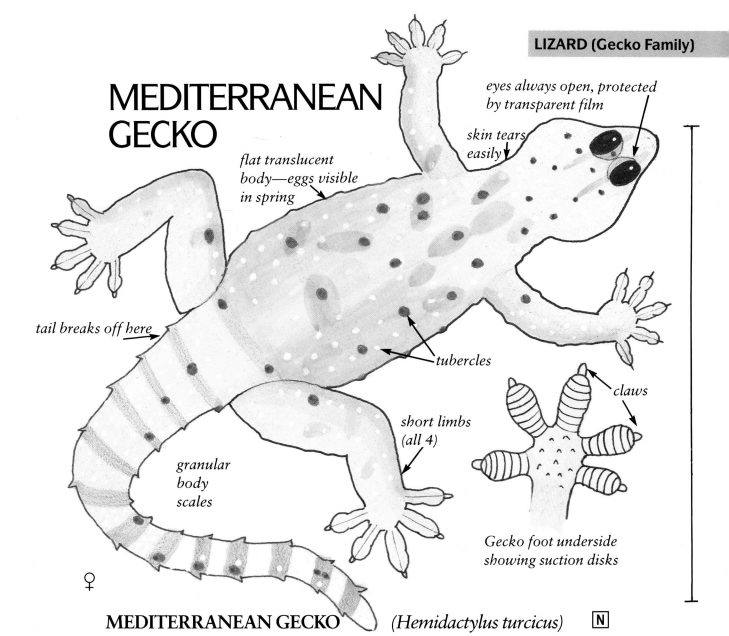

*eyes always open, protected
by transparent film*

*skin tears
easily*

*flat translucent
body—eggs visible
in spring*

tail breaks off here

tubercles

*short limbs
(all 4)*

*granular
body
scales*

claws

*Gecko foot underside
showing suction disks*

♀

MEDITERRANEAN GECKO *(Hemidactylus turcicus)* N

Grandmother's store-bought Mediterranean Gecko lost no time in getting down to work. Mediterranean Geckos are welcome guests in many subtropical homes because they help control annoying insect visitors. Geckos hunt at night, although once in a while a cheerful daytime chirp is heard. They are one of the few lizards with voices. Geckos are usually harmless, but look out for the Tokay Gecko *(Gekko gecko)* of Asia, which can inflict a painful bite. Geckos are amazing climbers. Their foot pads have suction disks (special plates with tiny, hooklike projections) that enable them to scurry up and down walls and across ceilings. The Mediterranean Gecko's tongue is used to pick up food and to wipe its lidless eyes to keep them clean and moist. There are hundreds of species of geckos in the world.

On a shelf
next to the jelly,
Grandma found
a big Bluebelly.

WESTERN FENCE LIZARD

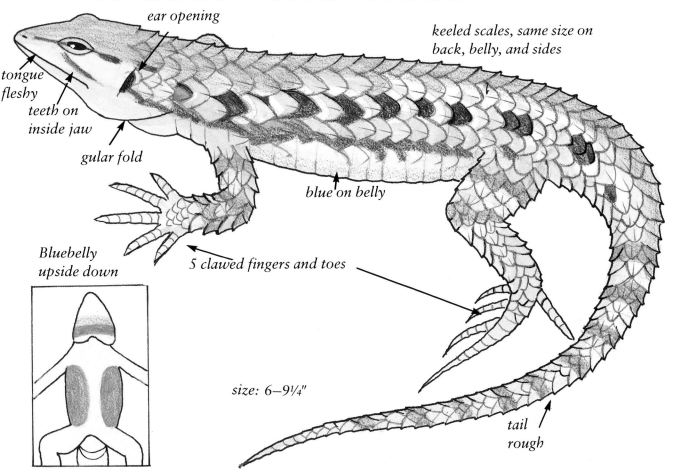

ear opening

keeled scales, same size on back, belly, and sides

tongue fleshy

teeth on inside jaw

gular fold

blue on belly

Bluebelly upside down

5 clawed fingers and toes

size: 6–9¼"

tail rough

WESTERN FENCE LIZARD (BLUEBELLY)
(Sceloporus occidentalis)

Ⓓ

The Western Fence Lizard that invaded Grandma's kitchen cabinet is also called a Bluebelly because of the blue patches on its underside. It is difficult to tell the difference between a lizard and a salamander. Both have long, slender bodies, long tails, and similar arms and legs, but only lizards have scaly skins, clawed feet, and external ear openings. The female Bluebelly lays up to 14 eggs. Western Fence Lizards live in and around fences and old buildings. Males display their bellies to attract females or to discourage other males from entering their territories. When a predator grabs a lizard's tail, it comes off, distracting the attacker and allowing the lizard to escape. A new tail (or tails) will grow to replace the lost one. The new tail is supported internally by cartilage rather than bone and will have a different coloration and texture.

A Whiptail chased
a falling petal
into an old
and rusty kettle.

WESTERN WHIPTAIL

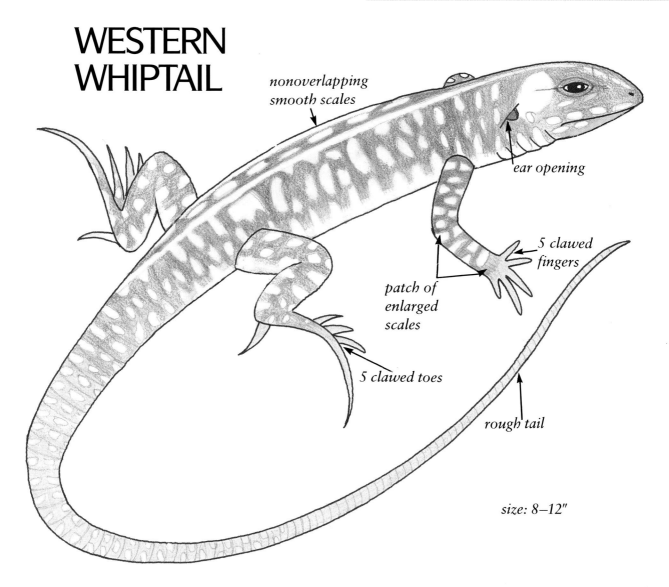

nonoverlapping smooth scales

ear opening

5 clawed fingers

patch of enlarged scales

5 clawed toes

rough tail

size: 8–12"

WESTERN WHIPTAIL *(Cnemidophorus tigris)*   D

Like the Western Whiptail under Nick's horse, most whiptails will chase almost anything small that moves. Whiptails, one of the fastest-moving lizards, come in a variety of patterns. The tail is especially long. The young Western Whiptail has a bright blue tail, which fades as it grows older. The whiptail, like most lizards, stays in the same area and rarely travels more than a few hundred feet during its lifetime. The Western Whiptail lays up to 4 eggs. Whiptails are currently being closely studied by herpetologists because some species are all female and lay fertile eggs without male fertilization. The eggs hatch into more female whiptails. Whiptails eat spiders, small scorpions, and insects.

A pocket is no place,
Sam thinks,
for Grant to carry
his pair of Skinks.

WESTERN SKINK

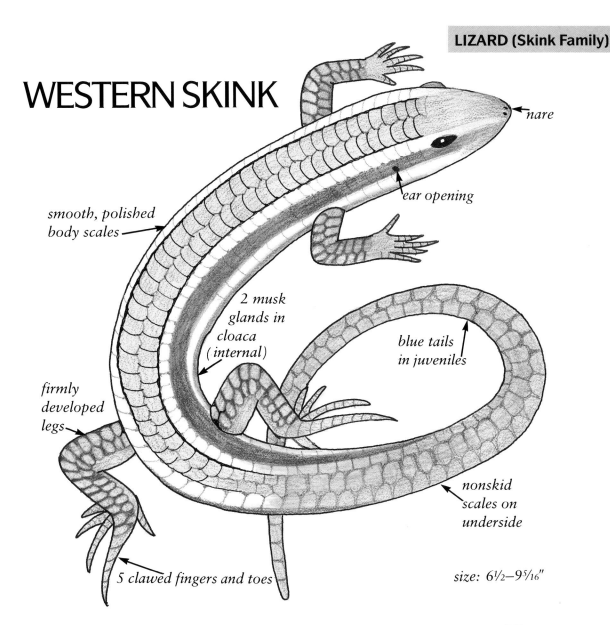

nare

ear opening

smooth, polished
body scales

2 musk
glands in
cloaca
(internal)

blue tails
in juveniles

firmly
developed
legs

nonskid
scales on
underside

5 clawed fingers and toes

size: 6½–9⁵⁄₁₆″

WESTERN SKINK (*Eumeces skiltonianus*) D

Grant put his Western Skinks into his pocket very carefully because their tails break off easily, and they have been known to bite. The vivid blue tail of the juvenile Western Skink is used to draw attackers away from the vulnerable body. There are 600 species of skinks in the world, 15 in the United States. Skinks look like snakes with legs. They are found in dry woods, under leaves and other plant debris, and near streams and moist places. Female skinks protect their nests, leaving only to eat or drink. The burrowing Mole Skink (*Eumeces egregius*) has a see-through window in its lower eyelid that allows it to see when its eyes are closed and even when it is underground. Skinks eat insects, worms, spiders, and small boneless animals.

How Frogs and Toads Grow

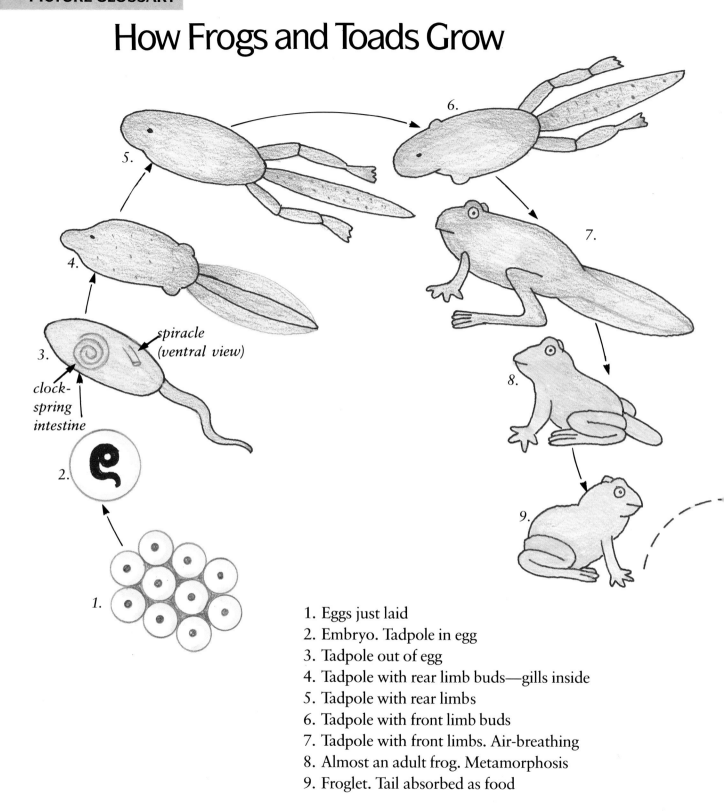

*spiracle
(ventral view)*

*clock-
spring
intestine*

1. Eggs just laid
2. Embryo. Tadpole in egg
3. Tadpole out of egg
4. Tadpole with rear limb buds—gills inside
5. Tadpole with rear limbs
6. Tadpole with front limb buds
7. Tadpole with front limbs. Air-breathing
8. Almost an adult frog. Metamorphosis
9. Froglet. Tail absorbed as food

From Egg to Froglet or Toadlet

TADPOLE TIMETABLE

Example	Tadpole stage
Bullfrog	2–3 years
Southern Leopard Frog	60–80 days
Southern Chorus Frog	50–60 days
Eastern Spadefoot Toad	14–60 days
American Toad	50–65 days
Oak Toad	30–60 days
Texas Toad	45–75 days

FROGLET OR TOADLET SIZE

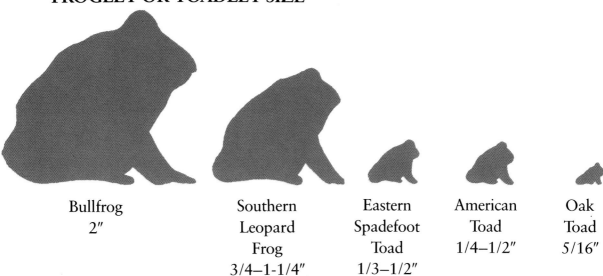

Bullfrog
2"

Southern
Leopard
Frog
3/4–1-1/4"

Eastern
Spadefoot
Toad
1/3–1/2"

American
Toad
1/4–1/2"

Oak
Toad
5/16"

Hibernation of Frogs and Toads

When winter arrives, northern frogs and toads need to hibernate to survive, as they are cold-blooded and would perish in freezing surface temperatures. Frogs burrow under mud or dead leaves in the bottom of a pond, or under rocks or rotten logs on land. Toads dig as deep as 1 foot down into the soil. In the desert, the opposite occurs. Frogs and toads burrow to avoid the summer heat, a process known as estivation.

Anatomy of Frog or Toad
(Class Amphibia)

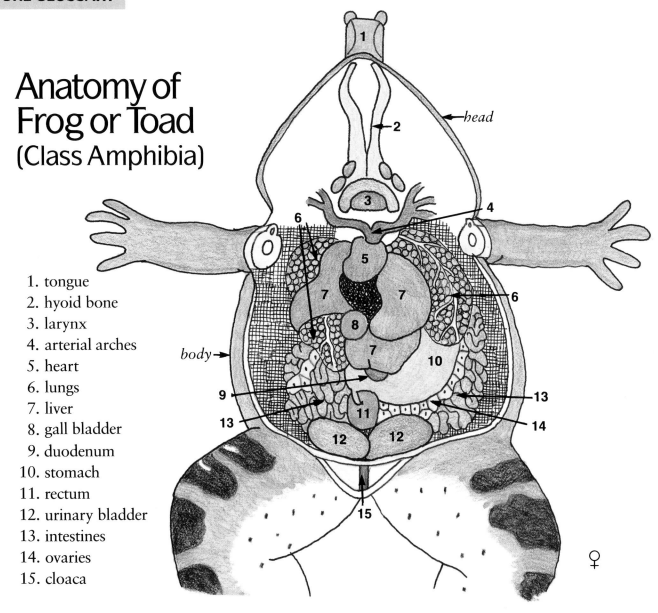

1. tongue
2. hyoid bone
3. larynx
4. arterial arches
5. heart
6. lungs
7. liver
8. gall bladder
9. duodenum
10. stomach
11. rectum
12. urinary bladder
13. intestines
14. ovaries
15. cloaca

VENTRAL VIEW (UNDERSIDE)

Amphibians have more primitive body structures than reptiles. They have 3-chambered hearts, breathe through their skins, change color for protection, and are cold-blooded. Toads and frogs have thin skulls, few bones, no tails, and no ribs. Their arms, legs, and internal ears are well developed. Frogs and toads have moist skins. Generally, frogs have smooth, soft skins; toads have rough, warty skins. Frog and toad females are often larger than the males and are voiceless except when alarmed.

Anatomy of Lizard
(Class Reptilia)

1. thyroid gland
2. vena cava
3. trachea
4. heart
5. lungs
6. liver
7. stomach (under liver)
8. gall bladder
9. eggs
10. intestines
11. oviduct
12. kidney
13. bladder
14. cloaca

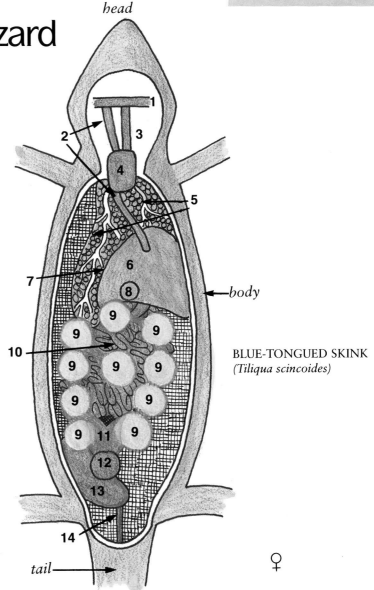

head

body

BLUE-TONGUED SKINK
(Tiliqua scincoides)

tail

♀

VENTRAL VIEW (UNDERSIDE)

Lizards' dry, scaly skins, enlarged and better developed lungs, external ears, and clawed feet differentiate them from salamanders. Typical lizards have long bodies, long legs, and long, thin tails. A few have round, fat bodies. Some have no legs at all. Lizards have teeth and are, except for the gecko, generally voiceless. They are cold-blooded and are closely related to snakes. The ability of lizards to lay eggs with shells on land puts them one step up the evolutionary ladder from amphibians, whose eggs, encased in jelly, are deposited in water.

Scalation of Lizard
(Class Reptilia)

VENTRAL VIEW (UNDERSIDE)

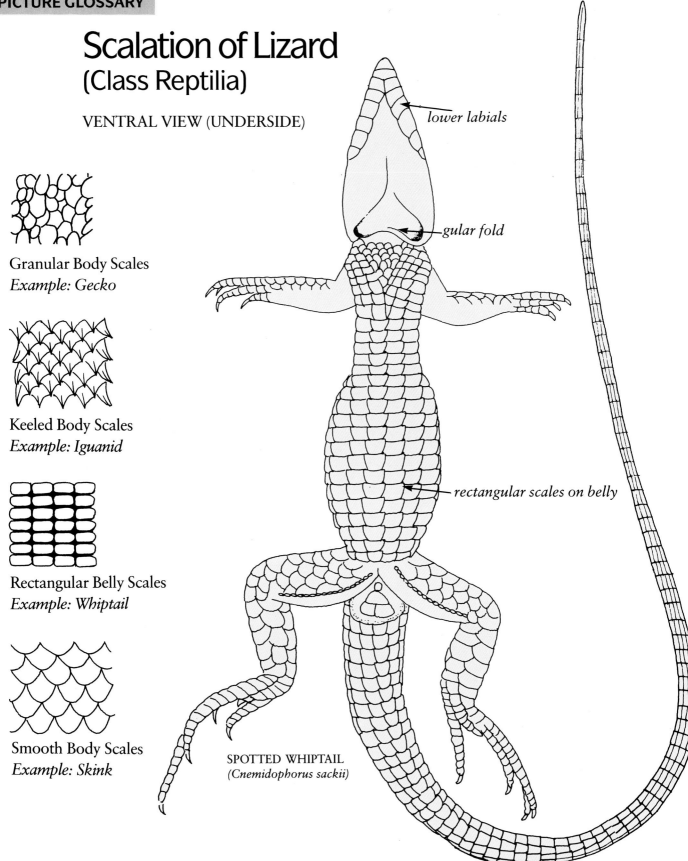

Granular Body Scales
Example: Gecko

Keeled Body Scales
Example: Iguanid

Rectangular Belly Scales
Example: Whiptail

Smooth Body Scales
Example: Skink

lower labials

gular fold

rectangular scales on belly

SPOTTED WHIPTAIL
(Cnemidophorus sackii)

Glossary

amphibian—a frog, toad, or salamander that typically lives in water during its early life and on land as an adult.

aquatic—living in water.

breeding—reproductive activities.

capillary action—the movement of liquid up or down on a groove or through a narrow tube. In a salamander, water moves up the costal grooves to moisten the skin.

cartilage—firm, elastic tissue, not quite a bone.

cloaca—the last chamber in an amphibian or reptile, into which digestive, urinary, and reproductive systems empty. The cloaca opens outside the animal through the anus.

clutch—a group; usually pertains to eggs.

cold-blooded—without internal mechanisms to regulate body temperature. Cold-blooded animals are never warmer than the air around them.

costal groove—a vertical groove on the side of a salamander.

cranial crest—a bony ridge over a toad's eye.

diurnal—active during the day.

dorsolateral fold—a crease at the area of body where back and sides meet.

embryo—in frogs and toads, the stage of development after the new-laid egg and before the tadpole.

evolution—any process of formation or growth.

fertile—capable of producing offspring or fruit.

fertilize—to make productive.

genus (plural, **genera**)—a division in the classification of plants and animals, containing one to several hundred species.

gills—organs used to breathe underwater.

gular fold—a skin fold at the throat of a lizard and salamander.

herpetologist—a person who studies reptiles and/or amphibians.

hibernate—to spend the winter in a dormant state.

keeled scale—a ridged scale found on some lizards.

labials—rows of scales above and below a reptile's mouth, important in the identification of species.

larva (plural, **larvae**)—the stage of life between the hatched egg and the adult.

mental gland—a gland on the chin of male lungless salamanders that secretes odors used in sex recognition.

metamorphosis—a stage of development from larva to adult; for example, when a tadpole becomes a frog or toad.

musk—a glandular secretion with a strong odor.

nare—a nostril opening.

nocturnal—active during the night.

paratoid gland—a gland on each side of the neck or behind the eye in toads and some salamanders.

pelvic region—the lower part of an animal's body associated with the lower limb girdle.

predator—an animal that hunts another animal for food.

regenerated—regrown.

sacral hump—the part of a frog's body where the backbone meets the lower limb girdle.

species—a further division of genus.

subspecies—a further division of species.

tadpole—the larval stage of a frog or toad.

terrestrial—living on the land.

translucent—permitting light to pass through but not transparent.

tubercles—warts or bumps.

tympanum—the external eardrum.

vena cava—two large veins that carry blood to the heart.

vent or **anus**—the place where the cloaca opens to the outside of the body.

vocal sac—a pouch on the throat of a male frog or toad that expands when the male is calling.

webbing—thin skin between the toes of frogs and toads.

Salamanders

Toads

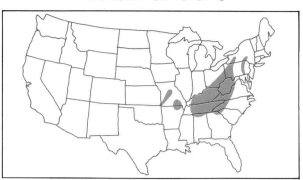

Hellbender

Eastern Spadefoot Toad

California Newt

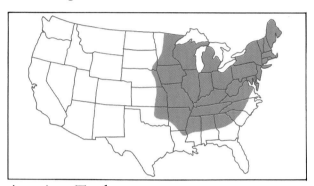

American Toad

Two-toed Amphiuma

Oak Toad

Ensatina (all subspecies)

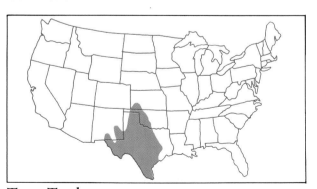

Texas Toad

These sixteen maps indicate distribution of the species in the United States only.

Frogs

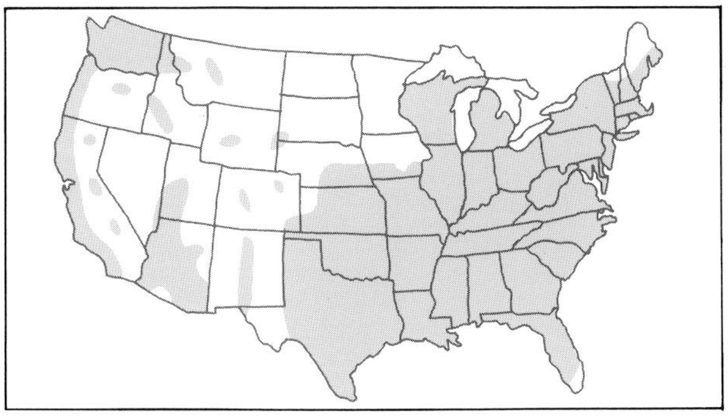

Bullfrog

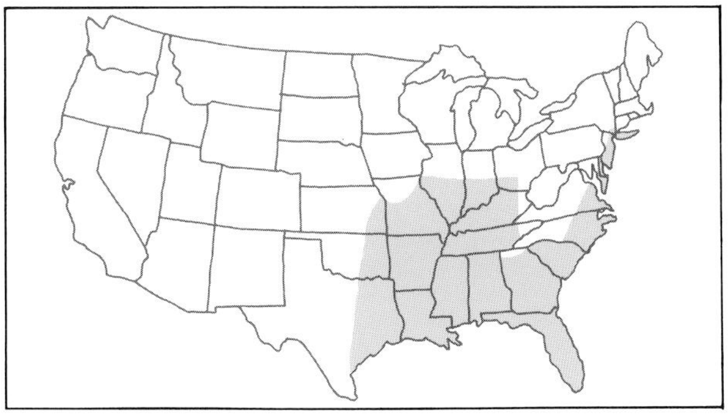

Southern Leopard Frog

Southern Chorus Frog

African Clawed Frog

Lizards

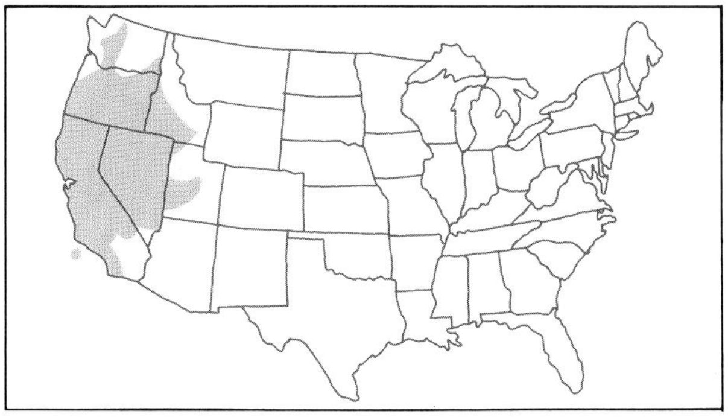

Western Fence Lizard

Mediterranean Gecko

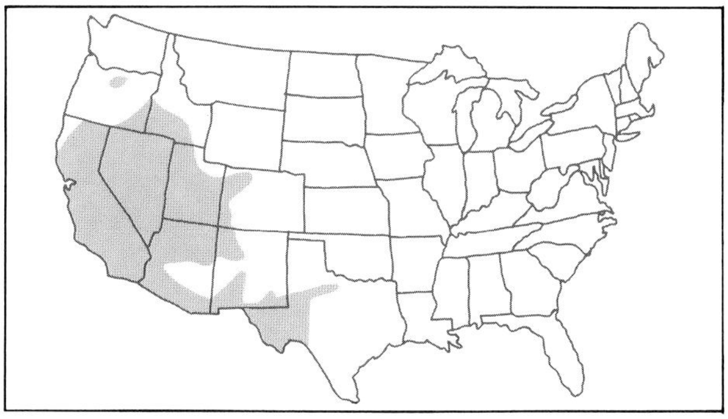

Western Whiptail

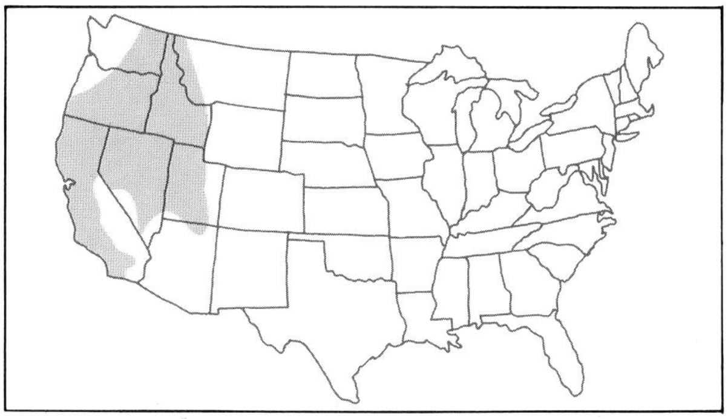

Western Skink

KINGDOM: ANIMAL

PHYLUM: CHORDATA

SUBPHYLUM: VERTEBRATA (segmented backbone)

Class	Order	Family (scientific & common name)	Example	Genus & species
Amphibia	Caudata	Cryptobranchidae — Giant Salamander	HELLBENDER	Cryptobranchus alleganiensis
Amphibia	Caudata	Salamandridae — Newt	CALIFORNIA NEWT	Taricha torosa
Amphibia	Caudata	Amphiumidae — Amphiuma	TWO-TOED AMPHIUMA	Amphiuma means
Amphibia	Caudata	Plethodontidae — Lungless Salamander	LARGE-BLOTCHED ENSATINA	Ensatina eschscholtzi klauberi
Amphibia	Salientia	Pelobatidae — Spadefoot Toad	EASTERN SPADEFOOT TOAD	Scaphiopus h. hollbrooki
Amphibia	Salientia	Bufonidae — Toad	AMERICAN TOAD	Bufo americanus
Amphibia	Salientia	Bufonidae — Toad	OAK TOAD	Bufo quercicus
Amphibia	Salientia	Bufonidae — Toad	TEXAS TOAD	Bufo speciosus
Amphibia	Salientia	Ranidae — True Frog	BULLFROG	Rana catesbeiana
Amphibia	Salientia	Ranidae — True Frog	SOUTHERN LEOPARD FROG	Rana utricularia
Amphibia	Salientia	Hylidae — Treefrog	SOUTHERN CHORUS FROG	Pseudacris nigrita
Amphibia	Salientia	Pipidae — Tongueless Frog	AFRICAN CLAWED FROG	Xenopus laevis
Reptilia	Squamata	Gekkonidae — Gecko	MEDITERRANEAN GECKO	Hemidactylus turcicus
Reptilia	Squamata	Iguanidae — Iguanid	WESTERN FENCE LIZARD	Sceloporus occidentalis
Reptilia	Squamata	Teiidae — Whiptail and Racerunner	WESTERN WHIPTAIL	Cnemidophorus tigris
Reptilia	Squamata	Scincidae — Skink	WESTERN SKINK	Eumeces skiltonianus

Bibliography

Behler, John L., and F. Wayne King. *The Audubon Society Field Guide to North American Reptiles and Amphibians*. New York: Knopf, 1979.

Breen, John F. *Encyclopedia of Reptiles and Amphibians*. Neptune, N.J.: T.F.T. Publications, 1974.

Carr, Archie. *The Reptiles*. New York: Time, Inc., 1963.

Cochran, Doris M. *Living Amphibians of the World*. New York: Doubleday, 1961.

Cole, Joanna. *A Frog's Body*. Photographs by Jerome Wexler. New York: Morrow, 1980.

Collins, Henry Hill, Jr. *Complete Field Guide to American Wildlife*. New York: Harper & Row, 1959.

Dickerson, Mary Cynthia. *The Frog Book: North American Toads and Frogs, with a Study of the Habits and Life Histories of Those of the Northeastern States*. Garden City, N.Y.: Doubleday, Page, 1908.

Encyclopedia of Reptiles, Amphibians and Other Cold-blooded Animals. London: Octopus, 1975.

Fogden, Michael and Patricia. *Animals and Their Colors: Camouflage, Warning Coloration, Courtship and Territorial Display, Mimicry*. New York: Crown, 1974.

Gilbert, Bil. "Lizards That Take to the Desert like Ducks to Water." *Smithsonian*, vol. 18, no. 5 (August 1987).

Grzimek, Bernhard. *Grzimek's Animal Life Encyclopedia*, vols. V, VI. New York: Van Nostrand Reinhold, 1974.

Halliday, Tim R., and Kraig Adler. *Encyclopedia of Reptiles and Amphibians*. New York: Facts on File, 1987.

Mertens, Robert. *The World of Amphibians and Reptiles*. New York: McGraw-Hill, 1960.

Storer, Tracy I., Robert C. Stebbins, Robert L. Usinger, and James W. Nybakken. *General Zoology*, 6th ed. New York: McGraw-Hill, 1979.

Wright, Albert H., and Anna A. Wright. *Handbook of Frogs and Toads of the U.S. and Canada*. Ithaca, N.Y.: Comstock, 1967.

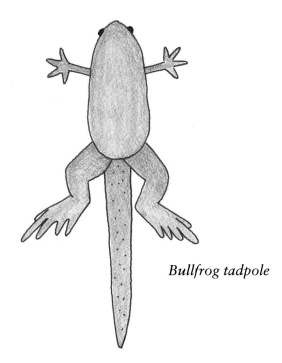

Bullfrog tadpole

47

Index